CLOTHING THEN AND NOW

by Nadia Higgins

pogo

Ideas for Parents and Teachers

Pogo Books let children practice reading informational text while introducing them to nonfiction features such as headings, labels, sidebars, maps, and diagrams, as well as a table of contents, glossary, and index.

Carefully leveled text with a strong photo match offers early fluent readers the support they need to succeed.

Before Reading

- "Walk" through the book and point out the various nonfiction features. Ask the student what purpose each feature serves.
- Look at the glossary together. Read and discuss the words.

Read the Book

- Have the child read the book independently.
- Invite him or her to list questions that arise from reading.

After Reading

- Discuss the child's questions. Talk about how he or she might find answers to those questions.
- Prompt the child to think more. Ask: Clothes and fashion trends have changed over time. What do you think will be a trend of the future?

Pogo Books are published by Jump!
5357 Penn Avenue South
Minneapolis, MN 55419
www.jumplibrary.com

Library of Congress Cataloging-in-Publication Data

Names: Higgins, Nadia, author.
Title: Clothing then and now / by Nadia Higgins.
Description: Minneapolis, MN: Jump!, Inc., [2019]
Series: Then and now | Audience: 7-10. | Includes index.
Identifiers: LCCN 2018026423 (print)
LCCN 2018038817 (ebook)
ISBN 9781641284677 (ebook)
ISBN 9781641284653 (hardcover : alk. paper)
ISBN 9781641284660 (pbk.)
Subjects: LCSH: Clothing and dress–History
Juvenile literature.
Fashion–History–Juvenile literature.
Classification: LCC GT518 (ebook)
LCC GT518 .H54 2019 (print) | DDC 391.009–dc23
LC record available at https://lccn.loc.gov/2018026423

Editor: Jenna Trnka
Designer: Molly Ballanger

Photo Credits: 123rf, cover (left); Ronnachai Palas/Shutterstock, cover (right); Monkey Business Images/Shutterstock, 1, 11; Ajintai/Shutterstock, 3; IanDagnall Computing/Alamy, 4; stockstudioX/iStock, 5; Andreas von Einsiedel/Getty, 6-7; wyrdlight/Alamy, 8-9; Dorling Kindersley ltd/Alamy, 9; trigga/iStock, 10; Chicago History Museum/Getty, 12-13; Hum Images/Alamy, 14-15; ClassicStock.com/SuperStock, 16; LE TELLIER Philippe/Getty, 17; Sophie BRAMLY/Getty, 18-19 (foreground); Bob Rowan/Getty, 18-19 (background); Rawpixel/iStock, 20-21; Nicole Hill Gerulat/Getty, 23.

Printed in the United States of America at Corporate Graphics in North Mankato, Minnesota.

TABLE OF CONTENTS

CHAPTER 1

THE ROLE OF CLOTHES

Clothes are a basic human need. They keep us warm. Long ago, people made clothes from plants and animals. They wove grasses into cloth. Some stayed warm in coats made of fur and animal skins.

fur coat

Today, we still need clothes that protect us. Against what? Sunshine. Rain. Cold temperatures.

Clothes can be clues. They can tell us about the people who wore them. In the 1700s, **wealthy** American **colonists** wore fancy gowns and suits. Made of what? Fine silk and lace. These materials were expensive. They were signs of wealth.

WHAT DO YOU THINK?

What materials are your clothes made of? Check the labels. What do you think your clothes say about you? Do they say anything about where you live? How so?

lace

People use clothing to show their **style**. In the 1850s, huge skirts were the **fashion**. Women had a trick for making their skirts pouf. They wore crinolines. These were worn under skirts. They held the skirts out wide.

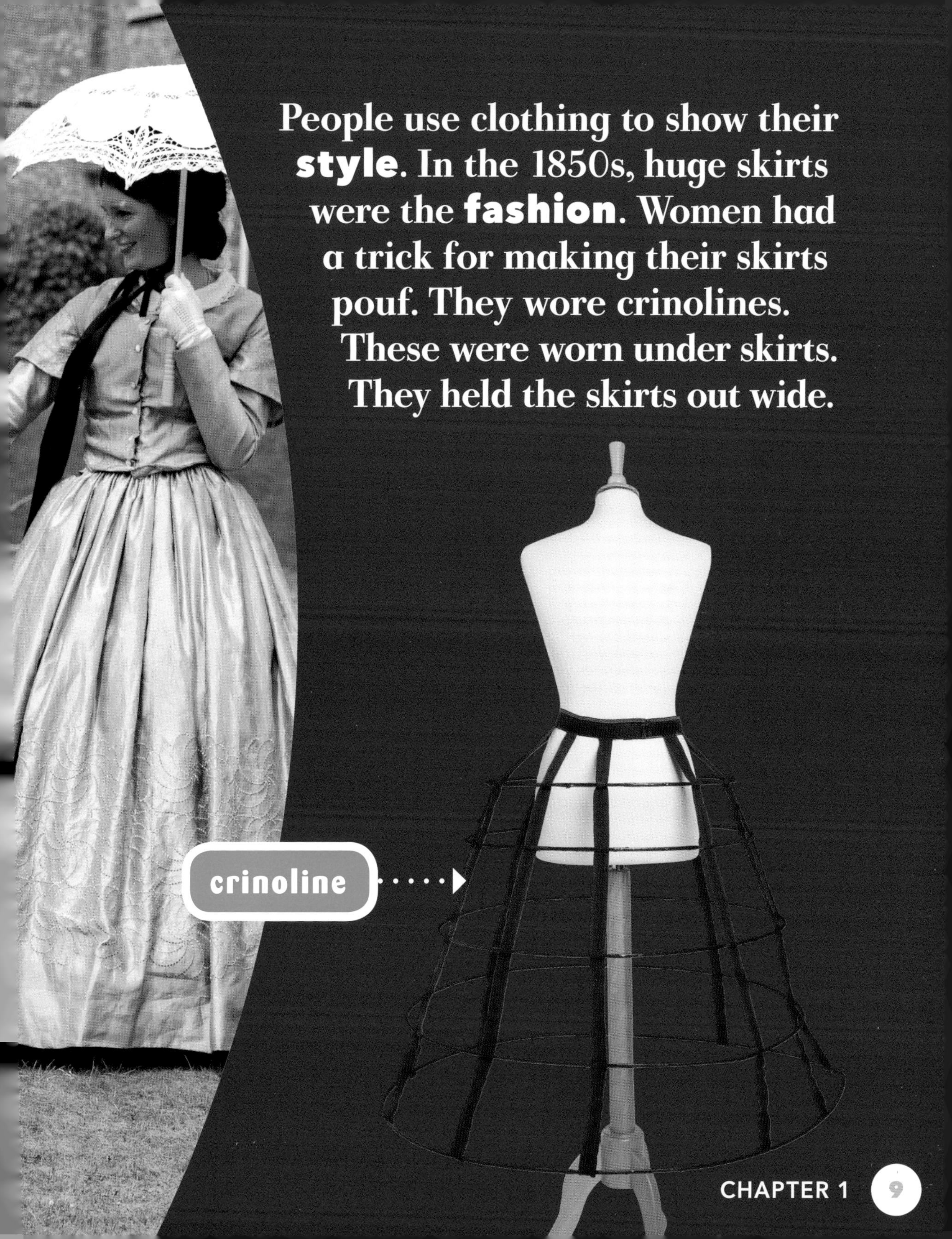

CHAPTER 2

BE PRACTICAL

In 1873, blue jeans were invented. For what? Wearing to work. These denim pants were made to be tough. **Rivets** were added to make them stronger.

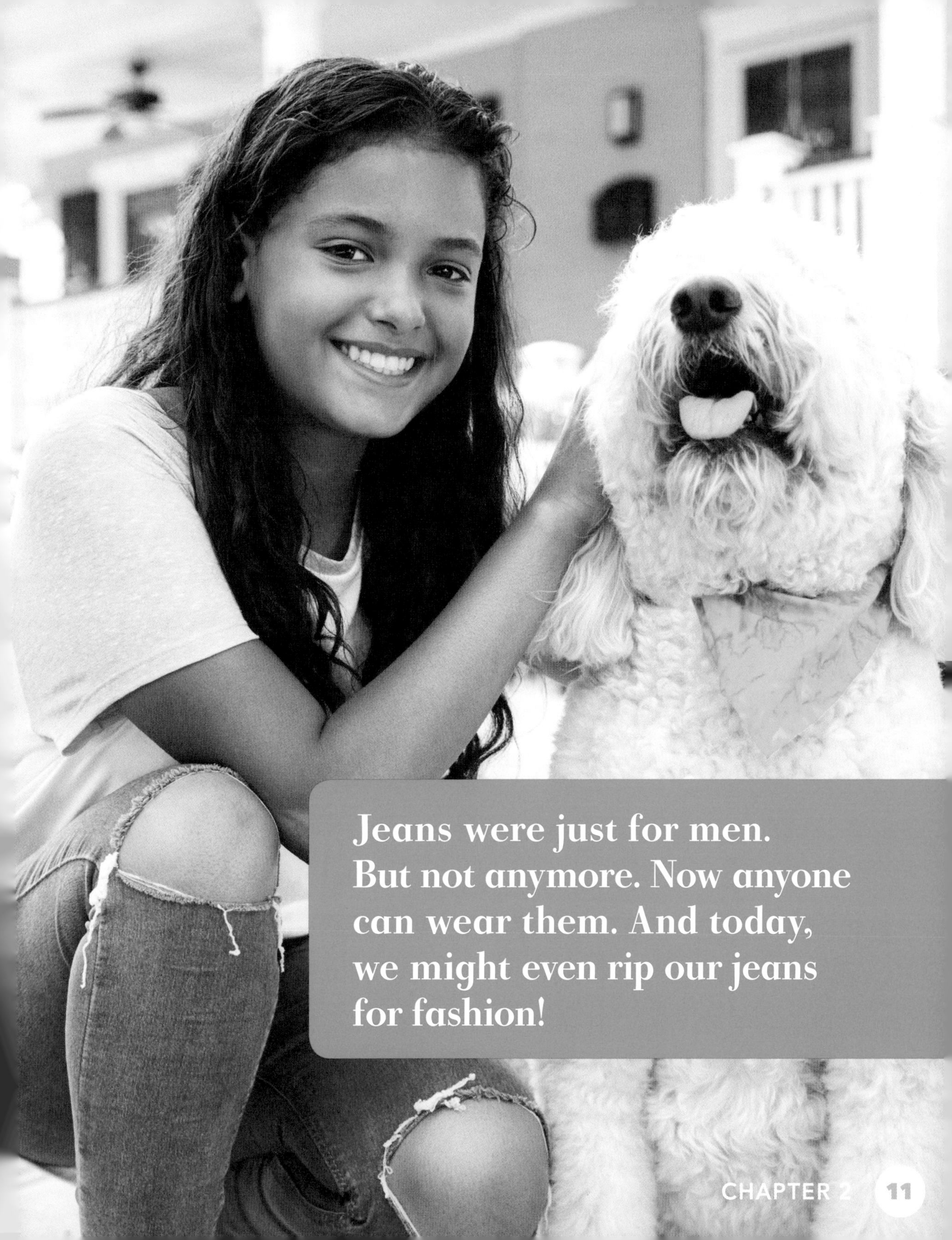

Jeans were just for men. But not anymore. Now anyone can wear them. And today, we might even rip our jeans for fashion!

By the 1920s, new inventions changed clothing. Sewing machines. Zippers. New kinds of fabric. Clothes got more comfortable. **Mass production** made them more affordable. A person did not have to be wealthy to look stylish.

TAKE A LOOK!

In the 1920s, young women created a daring new look. These women were called flappers. Their style told the world that they were fun and free.

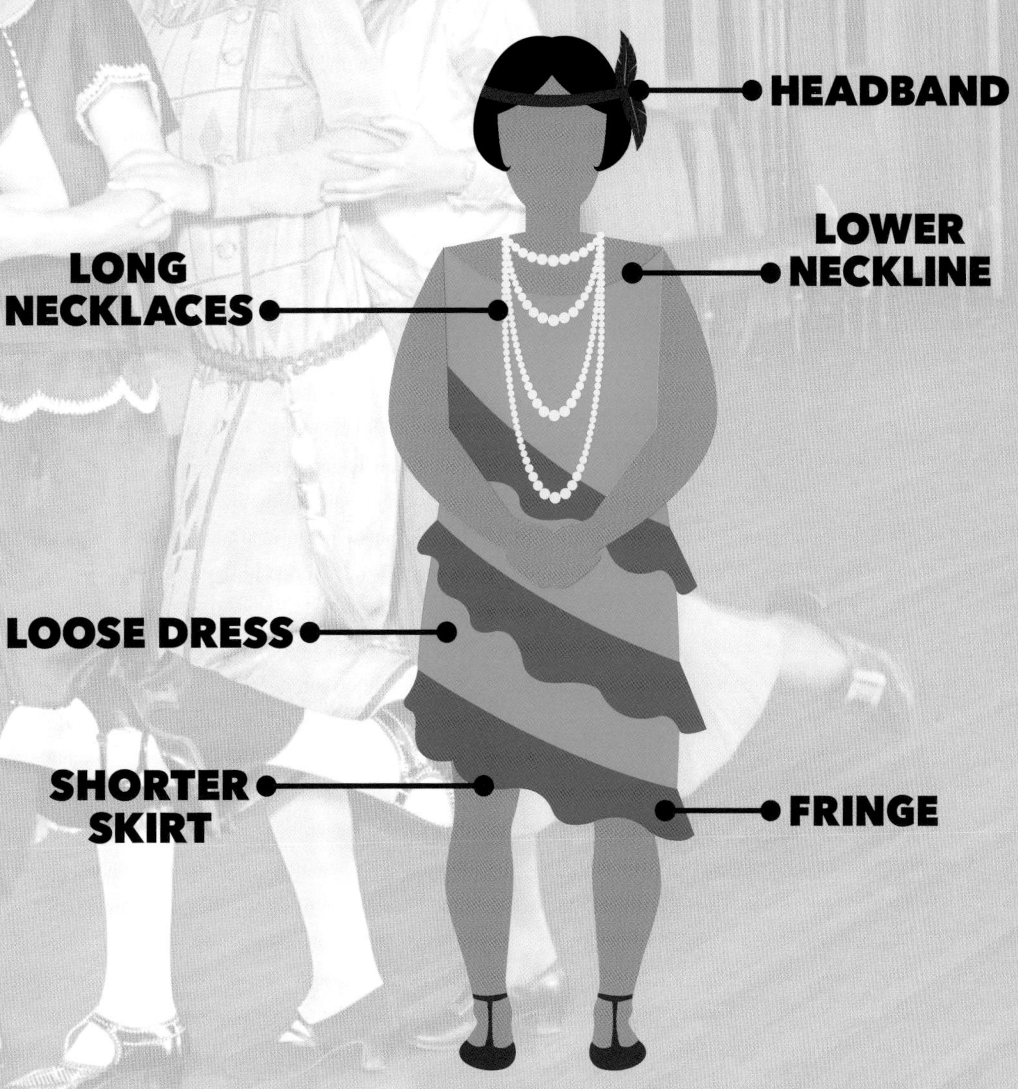

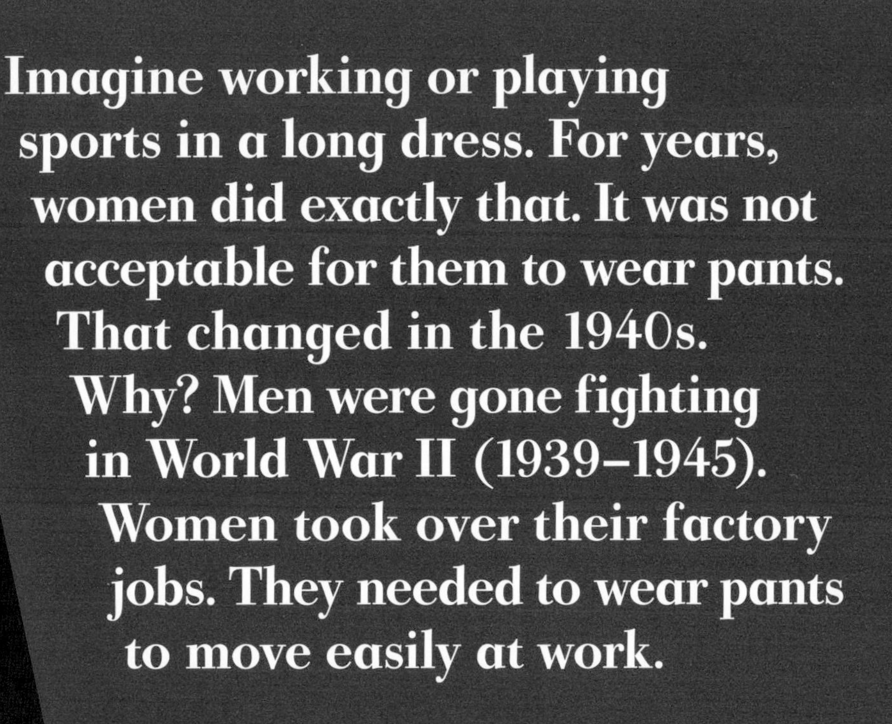

Imagine working or playing sports in a long dress. For years, women did exactly that. It was not acceptable for them to wear pants. That changed in the 1940s. Why? Men were gone fighting in World War II (1939–1945). Women took over their factory jobs. They needed to wear pants to move easily at work.

DID YOU KNOW?

At first, many women wore men's pants. As demand grew, pants were **tailored** to better fit women. Extra-large pockets helped women hold tools on the job.

CHAPTER 3

TRENDS THROUGH TIME

In the 1950s, teens began creating their own style. Poodle skirts were all the rage. They were worn with cardigan sweaters. Bobby socks. Saddle shoes.

In the 1960s and 1970s, **hippies** rejected the **trends** being set by the rest of the country. This was reflected in their clothing. They wore swirling colors and flowing fabrics.

In the 1980s, music videos took off. Video stars spread trends faster than ever. Leg warmers. Large jackets. Bright neon colors. All of these **fads** together created the look of the 1980s.

WHAT DO YOU THINK?

Funky. Cool. Preppy. These words can describe style. What is your style? How do you show it?

In the past, people may have owned just one or two outfits. Today, we might have choices for every activity. Why? Factories make clothes quickly. And at low cost. We are free to invent our own style. What will you wear next?

TAKE A LOOK!

Different **cultures** are a strong part of America's history. Including their clothing and fashion styles. Take a look at a few!

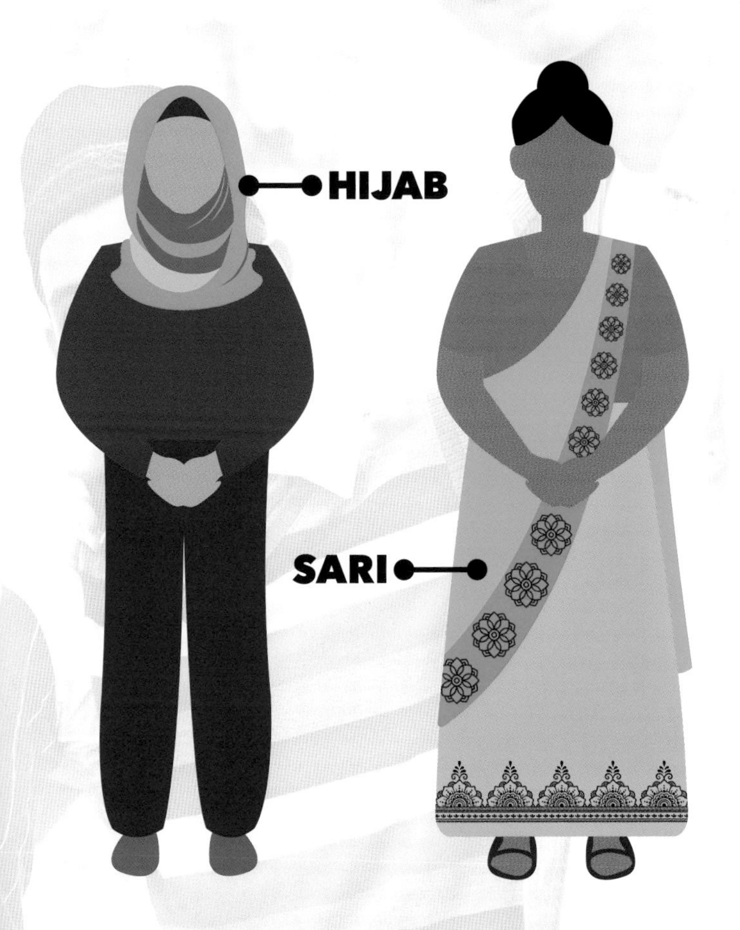

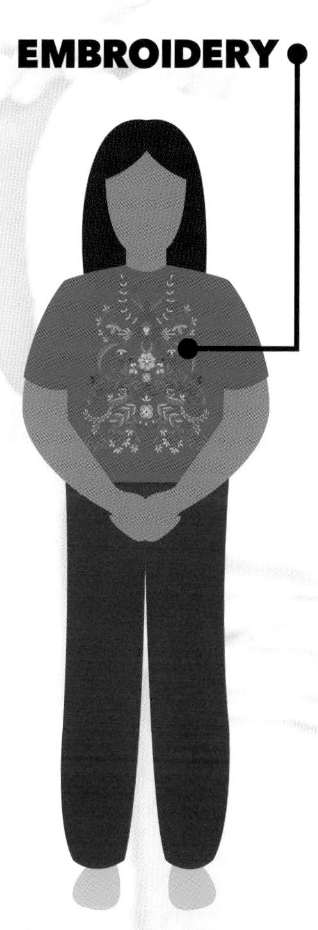

origin: Various countries with **Muslim** populations, such as Turkey, Egypt, and Iran

origin: India

origin: Mexico

ACTIVITIES & TOOLS

TRY THIS!

MAKE A FASHION COLLAGE

Make your own fashion rules by creating a fashion collage!

What You Need:

- fashion magazines
- scissors
- glue
- large sheet of paper
- markers

❶ Flip through the magazines. Cut out pictures of clothes that catch your eye.

❷ Arrange the pictures into outfits on the sheet of paper. Mix and match the clothes. What looks fun, interesting, and new?

❸ When you like the arrangements of the outfits, glue the pictures onto the sheet of paper.

❹ Use markers to add finishing touches. Add hats, belts, jewelry, and shoes. This is fashion. Make it your own!

GLOSSARY

colonists: The people who helped form the original 13 colonies of the United States.

cultures: The ideas, customs, traditions, and ways of life of groups of people.

fads: Things that are very popular for a short time.

fashion: A style or piece of clothing that is popular at a certain time.

hippies: Young people in the 1960s and 1970s who rejected traditional values.

mass production: The method of making large amounts of identical things with machines in a factory.

Muslim: People whose religion is Islam.

rivets: Short metal pins designed to hold something together.

style: The way in which people dress and act.

tailored: Fashioned or fitted.

trends: The newest fashions or styles that are popular at a certain time.

wealthy: To have a lot of money, property, or possessions.

INDEX

TO LEARN MORE

Finding more information is as easy as 1, 2, 3.

1. Go to www.factsurfer.com
2. Enter "clothingthenandnow" into the search box.
3. Click the "Surf" button to see a list of websites.